AF323628

AN OLD OTTAWA SQUAW AND WIGWAM

THE OTTAWAN

A SHORT HISTORY OF THE VILLAGES AND RESORTS SURROUNDING LITTLE TRAVERSE BAY, AND THE INDIAN LEGENDS CONNECTED THEREWITH

ALSO AN ACCOUNT OF THE NOTED MORMON KINGDOM ON BEAVER ISLAND DURING THE FIFTIES, BY ONE OF KING STRANG'S SONS, AND A "WRITE-UP" OF ANTIQUATED CROSS VILLAGE AND ITS FAMOUS CONVENT, NOW A THING OF THE PAST

ILLUSTRATED

BY

J. C. WRIGHT

1895

ROBERT SMITH & CO., PUBLISHERS AND PRINTERS
LANSING, MICHIGAN

S.B.N. 0-912382-31-7

L.O.C. 84-70899

Reprinted 1984

By

BLACK LETTER PRESS

Cover art: Robert Nelson

GREETING

HUNDREDS of the tourists who annually visit the Little Traverse region know that it is full of historical and legendary interest, but from the difficulty of obtaining the legends and information regarding its history many of them return to their homes without being able to appreciate the real charms of the region they have visited. For this reason especially have I written THE OTTAWAN, hoping that it may prove a worthy memento of one of the oldest missionary fields in the northwest and one of the fairest spots on the entire globe.

For my historical information I am greatly indebted to Dr. M. L. Leach's History of the Grand Traverse Region.

I take pleasure in calling the attention of my readers to that portion of the work devoted to the Mormon kingdom on Beaver Island, for which I am indebted to Mr. Chas. J. Strang, of Lansing, Mich., one of King Strang's sons. I believe it to be correct in every particular.

I am also under obligations to Mr. Thos. T. Bates, editor of the Grand Traverse Herald, Traverse City, Mich., and Mr. Andrew J. Blackbird, and Rev. Father Zephryn, Harbor Springs, Mich.

J. C. WRIGHT.

Harbor Springs, June, 1895.

LITTLE TRAVERSE BAY

LITTLE TRAVERSE BAY is an indentation of the eastern shore of northern Lake Michigan. It is nine miles long and with a width of six miles at its mouth, its shores gradually approach each other until only two miles apart, forming the "Head of the Bay" into a semicircle.

The name "Little Traverse" originated with the early French *voyageurs* who discovered and named two indentations of the coast line, *La Petit Travers* and *La Grande Travers*, now known as Little Traverse and Grand Traverse Bays.

By the Indians, Little Traverse Bay was called "We-kwa-don-sing," which means "the little bay." By degrees that name was restricted to the harbor on the north side of the bay, and finally it was appropriated by an adjacent resort and changed by English pronunciation to We-que-ton-sing.

The bay is one of the most beautiful sheets of water to be found on the western continent. Poets and artists alike have tried in vain to paint its charms. To be appreciated it must be seen and then the human tongue utterly fails in language with which to describe the beauties of the scene. One writer in trying to describe his experience, says: "We took a little walk upon the bluffs this morning and looked out upon the panorama which nature, the great artist, spread before us. How can we describe, or how can the genius of man even attempt to portray the majesty of the Creator here made manifest? Could we but paint the beauty of the landscape spread out before us, the silver expanse of the bay, gemmed in her emerald setting, not of one green tint, but a thousand shades of variegated loveliness, from which the sun's soft rays come stealing in thankful benediction to soothe the weary brain and give the tired mortal heavenly rest, dotted here and there with steaming palaces and white sails, and just beyond, the wave crowned waters of old Michigan! Here indeed is nature in all her glorious reality, and we need ask no prophetic visions of the misty past nor revelations of the uncertain future to teach us of the tender loving care of our great father, God."

Volumes could be printed of such tributes made to the bay by enraptured visitors, but aside from its natural beauties, the Little Traverse region has a charm for all true lovers of American history, since it has been a field of almost continual missionary operations since the time of the illustrious Pere Marquette. Scenes similar to those connected with early missionary work in all parts of the new world have been enacted at Little Traverse Bay. Here Indian massacres and wars have occurred; early explorers and others have met their deaths at the stake within the sound of its breakers; numerous tribes have held great counsels on its shores, and hundreds of natives have been converted to the Christian faith and baptized in its blue waters.

EARLY MOVEMENTS OF THE INDIANS.

According to the Ottawa traditions, the first people to have inhabited the shores of Little Traverse Bay was a small tribe of Indians of western origin, known as the Mush-quah-tas, who resided between the present village of Harbor Springs and Seven Mile Point. They were afterwards conquered and driven southward by the Ottawas under the leadership of their famous chief, Sagama.

The origin of the Ottawas, as a tribe, as Dr. Leach tells us, "is veiled in the obscurity of the past."

They were a branch of the Algonquin family and formerly came from the east. The migration is supposed to have been caused by their powerful and warlike neighbors, the Iroquois. They came by the way of Canada, navigating the river which bears their name, and for a long time making their home on the Great Manitoulin Island in Lake Huron. At the Sault Ste. Marie they met the Chippewas, who then inhabited portions of the upper peninsula of Michigan, and as they resembled each other very much in language and customs, they formed a warm friendship which has never yet been broken. Together the two tribes journeyed toward the south and pitched their tents in the Grand and Little Traverse regions. At first they did not molest the peaceful Mush-quah-tas, but with other tribes they were continually at war. This sort of warlike life was disdainful to the Mush-quah-tas, however, and one day as the Ottawas were returning from a long expedition against the Sacs in Wisconsin, lamenting the loss of many braves, the Mush-quah-tas foolishly made fun of them and pelted them with chips and balls of ashes. From this insult the proud Ottawas could not recover, and when night drew on they mustered their warriors and attacked the Mush-quah-tas village.

The following graphic account of this battle is taken from Dr. Leach's History of the Grand Traverse Region, published in the Grand Traverse Herald in 1883:

"It may have been that a calm summer's night had nearly passed away. The first faint glimmering of light in the east heralds the approach of morn. The village of the Mush-quah-tas is still wrapt in slumber. The sleeping mother gently clasps her baby to her breast, unconscious of approaching danger. The maiden dreams of her lover; the young man of glorious feats of the chase or of war. The old brave lives over again the experiences of his youth or dreams of the happy hunting ground to which he is hastening. Dark forms, crouching in the shadows, are stealthily approaching. On this side a long line of Ottawa braves, on that their friends and allies, the Chippewas. The lines close round the doomed village. Some of the crouching figures are already at the very doors. So noiseless and stealthily has been the approach that not even the watchful dogs have been alarmed. Suddenly there bursts upon the night air a sound to make the blood curdle—a deafening chorus of demoniac yells, as if uttered in concert by a legion of frantic furies. Full well the startled Mush-quah-tas know the fearful import of that sound, the war-whoop of their enemies. Full well they know there is no avoiding the death struggle. The old brave reaches for his war club and the young man strings his bow, but their assailants are quick and powerful, and the stone hatchets are wielded with terrible effect. Crushed and mangled, they go down, slain, but not conquered. The maiden covers her face with her garment, and quietly bows her head to the fatal blow. The mother loosens her clasp of her frightened infant, seizes the nearest weapon, and with the fierceness of a tigress at bay, springs upon her foes. Her blows tell, but fierceness can not long avail against strength and numbers. She falls mortally wounded. Her dying eyes are turned lovingly upon her child. A brawny warrior seizes it by the feet, whirls it high in air, dashes it with crushing force upon the earth, and flings its bleeding and lifeless body upon its mother's bosom. The surprised Mush-quah-tas, taken at a disadvantage, make a brave fight, but victory does not long waver in the balance. As the sun rises upon the scene, all the inmates save one of that doomed village lie stark and bleeding on the ground, or are consuming in the rapidly burning wigwams. The revenge of the insulted Ottawas is complete."

According to the Ottawa tradition this was the most terrible battle ever fought in this region. Only one man escaped who carried the news of the disaster to an old man and his family who had suspected danger and fled down the coast, taking up their temporary abode near the present site of the village of Harbor Springs. These, together with the remnants of the tribe from a few small outlying villages, journeyed southward and established themselves near the St. Joseph River. Later they suffered a second crushing defeat from the Ottawas from the effects of which they never recovered. The Mush-quah-tas had incurred the enmity of a powerful tribe and they paid the penalty with their lives.

The descendants of the conquering Ottawas and Chippewas have resided on and about the shores of Little Traverse Bay ever since. They are not all pure Ottawas, as is often thought, but a mixture of the Ottawas and Chippewas, though they talk the Ottawa language.

Some time after Father Marquette's Huron settlement at Point St. Ignace left for Detroit in 1702, the numbers of the Ottawas in the Little Traverse region were greatly augmented by the arrival of the Ottawa village from West Moran Bay.

Some idea of the habits and customs of these Indians, when they were first visited by the whites, can be obtained from an article written by Father Menard, one of the early missionaries who labored so zealously and who endured so many hardships to spread the gospel among the Indians of this region.   He says:

"There is here a false and abominable religion similar in many things to that of some ancient pagans.   The Indians here do not acknowledge any sovereign Maker of Heaven and earth.   They believe that there are many manitous, some of whom are beneficent, as the sun, the moon, the lake, the river and woods; others malevolent, as for instance, snakes, dragons, cold, storms; and, in general, all that appears to them useful or injurious, they call a manitou, and they render to such objects the worship and veneration which we give to the true God alone. They invoke them when they go to hunt, to fish, to war or on a voyage.   *   * I have seen an idol set up in the middle of a village, to which, among other presents, they offered ten dogs in sacrifice that this false god might vouchsafe to banish elsewhere a malady which was depopulating the village.   *   *   *   During storms and tempests they sacrifice a dog to the lake, which they throw into the water saying: 'Here is something to pacify thee; be still!' * * * For the rest, as these people are dull, they do not acknowledge any deity purely spiritual. They believe that the sun is a man, and the moon is his wife; that snow and ice are also human beings, who go away in spring and come back again in winter; that the devil dwells in snakes, dragons and other monsters; that crows, hawks and some other birds are manitous, and talk as well as we do, pretending there are some Indians who understand their language, just as some of them understand a little French. Moreover, they believe that the souls of the departed govern the fishes of the lake, and hence, at all times, they have believed in the immortality of the soul, even holding the doctrine of metempsychosis—that is the transmigration of the souls of deceased fishes, for they believe that they again pass into the bodies of other fishes. For this reason they never throw the remains of fish they have eaten into the fire for fear of displeasing the shades of those fishes, so that they might not come into their nets any more."

Nothing further of importance is known in regard to the early history of the Ottawas, living strictly in the Little Traverse region. During their uncivilized state they were always engaged in battle with other tribes of Indians and they frequently carried their warfare far into the heart of their enemies' country. They were connected with Pontiac's conspiracy, he himself being an Ottawa, and they made a formidable foe to the Americans in the war of 1812. Some of the greatest Indian chiefs on the American continent wore the war paint and feathers of the Ottawas. But though they were very warlike and superstitious during their wild state, these Indians have shown superiority over other tribes since the advent of civilization in this country. They easily learned to speak the English language and readily accepted the manners and customs of the paleface. They generally listened attentively to the teachings of the early missionaries, through whose efforts much was done toward their civilization, and the remnant tribes are rather more enlightened than the Indian is generally depicted on the average mind.

A LEGEND OF
LITTLE TRAVERSE BAY

MANY moons ago, when the Indians chased the deer through this then wild territory, and the squaws rocked their papooses to sleep 'neath the shade of the sheltering pines, there dwelt on the banks of Little Traverse Bay a peaceful band of Ottawas, who delighted more in the chase than in unfriendly encounters with neighboring tribes. They were presided over by Ma-gee-we-non, a great warrior and hunter, and for years they had dwelt in peace upon these shores, nothing ever occurring to mar their happiness, for they greatly loved their chief.

During his peaceful reign, a son was born to Ma-gee-we-non, which was his father's joy and pride. With the greatest delight the old chief spent most of his time teaching his boy to shoot the arrow and throw the spear, and making him acquainted with all the knowledge necessary to any Indian brave's education. But in spite of all that was done to make the young man a great chief, he early evinced traits of a diabolical character; although an adept in the use of his weapons, it became apparent that he was possessed of the evil spirit. He grew to large and ungainly proportions and became a human monstrosity. He delighted in torturing his people and did all sorts of things to annoy them. The following is an example of this fiend's machinations:

One day while out fishing, not being able to catch anything, he became angry and sought the feeding ground of the dreaded sea serpent, which he captured and turned loose in the village of his people, where the enraged reptile killed many of the inhabitants and committed all sorts of depredations.

The people in horror, called this evil man Motchimanitou (devil), and his father, Ma-gee-we-non, seeing his son's fate, killed himself in despair.

Finally, the people saw that in order to insure their safety, they must get rid of this Motchimanitou. A great council was held and the warriors turned out *en masse* to get him, dead or alive. But of no avail. He seemed to possess a charmed life. He never could be seen, but each morning the inhabitants would wake to find some new mischief but no signs of the perpetrator.

At last, after many days of searching, he was discovered, nestled among some sand dunes on the shore, fast asleep. Without losing any time the natives bound him with wampum ropes and when he awoke he was helpless. His captors placed him in a canoe and taking him far out into the bay tied huge stones to his neck and threw him overboard. But the end was not yet. As he reached the water, by his exertions to get loose, he caused such a sea that the canoe was upset and all its occupants drowned.

Thus ends the story of the Motchimanitou. Whether it be true or not remains a mystery, but at the head of the bay there lie six sand hills in such a position that the valleys between them form the perfect mold of a man—the place where the Indians claim the Motchimanitou was asleep when captured, and to the present day, when great tempests rage at sea, they say: "Oh, it's only Motchimanitou trying to get out of the water."

HARBOR SPRINGS FROM THE WEST, AND HARBOR POINT

L'ARBRE CROCHE MISSION

(HARBOR SPRINGS)

WHO the first explorer was that entered Little Traverse Bay is not definitely known. It was probably one of the early French *voyageurs* who traded with the Indians of the Mackinac country. Perhaps Nicholas Perrot, who stayed at Mackinac Island about 1665 and who made frequent visits along the coast in different directions, was the discoverer of *La Petit Travers*.

It was about the time of Pere Marquette's residence at Point St. Ignace, however, that the first mission was established on the shores of Little Traverse Bay, although by whom it was established is not known. Father Marquette went to St. Ignace in the spring of 1671 with the Huron Indians who were driven away from the mission of the Holy Ghost at La Pointe de St. Esprit, Chequamegon Bay, at the western extremity of Lake Superior, by the Nadouessi, a war-like tribe of Indians who inhabited the banks of the Mississippi river.

The mission at Little Traverse Bay may have been established by Frather Dablon, who built a chapel at Michilimackinac the winter before Marquette's* arrival there.

Whether there was a resident priest at the mission at the start we cannot ascertain, but if there was he probably did not remain any great length of time. In 1695 we find that it used to be attended by the Fathers stationed at Mackinaw, and the baptismal records are still preserved at St. Ignace. The first entries are of 1741, and the last of 1765, by Father du Jaunay, acting Cure of Michilimackinac.

Probably the reason that there was no resident priest at Little Traverse Bay is because there were not so many Indians at that point as at the other missions. However, the number steadily increased, as the surroundings were favorable.

*There is nothing to prove that Father Marquette was ever at Little Traverse Bay, but there is certainly no record to prove that he was not, and it is quite probable that he was, as it is not far distant from Point St. Ignace, where he resided for a considerable length of time, and there was a large number of Indians then residing at the bay.

Fish and game were abundant, and many of the Indians had fields of corn. They were also very ingenious and made baskets, mats and bags from the bark of the basswood tree, which were handsomely colored with dyes they manufactured from different roots and barks they found in the vicinity. They also made many useful articles from birch bark. But though they were somewhat more advanced than other nomadic tribes, they were very superstitious. Seven miles west of the mission, on the banks of a small stream, was a large wooden idol, painted and bedecked with feathers and other finery, which they worshipped and to which they offered sacrifices. This was as late as Father Baraga's time in 1831–2. The chapel was located on the north side of the bay, at the present site of the Catholic church at Harbor Springs, and was known as L'Arbre Croche mission. L'Arbre Croche village proper was located about thirteen miles further up the coast and at one time was the largest Indian village south of the Straits of Mackinac. It was at that point where the Menominees, Chippewas and Ottawas held council, in July of 1763, after the massacre of Fort Michilimackinac, *when

---

* Some historians claim that the name of the chief who presided over the Indians of L'Arbre Croche at the time of the council is not known, but Dr. Leach informs us that it was Ne-saw-kee, a great Ottawa, whose great grandson, Ne-se-wa-quat, still resides in Harbor Springs and is the rightful chief of the Ottawas.

the Ottawas had with them several English prisoners. The name is of French origin meaning "the crooked tree" and was given to the place on account of a large distorted pine tree which grew near by. The name was sometimes applied to the entire western coast of Emmet County, south of Cross Village.

After the time of Father du Jaunay the L'Arbre Croche Indians seem to have been left to themselves, though they may have been occasionally visited by a priest.

In 1825 Rev. Father Peter De Jean, arrived in the Little Traverse region and built a church at Seven Mile Point, but as it proved unsatisfactory, the mission was moved to the site of the old L'Arbre Croche mission, where a little log church was built by Father De Jean in 1827. During his stay at the new L'Arbre Croche mission Father De Jean conducted a day school for Indian children.

On the 21st of April, 1821, the mission was taken charge of by Father Baraga, who arrived from Cincinnati. A few weeks later Bishop Fenwick arrived and installed the zealous priest as pastor. "Happy day!" says he, writing to the Leopoldin Society, "happy day, which has placed me in the midst of the wild Indians, with whom I will stay, if it be the will of God, until the last breath of my life."

He was well liked by all the Indians and held services in the little church morning and night. He was assisted by an Indian chief, who read aloud from an Indian prayer book. Father Baraga lived in the greatest poverty. His pastoral residence was a rude log hut covered with bark, and when it rained he was compelled to spread his cloak over his books and papers to keep them from getting wet, but it is said of him that he felt happier than a millionaire in his palace. During his stay at the L'Arbre Croche mission he baptized 461 Indians. In 1832 he printed an Ottawa prayer and hymn book. He left the mission in 1833 and afterwards labored at different points on the upper peninsula. In 1853 he was consecrated Bishop of Sault Ste. Marie, the L'Arbre Croche Mission then being in his diocese.

A long list of priests succeeded him at the L'Arbre Croche mission, Father Pierz and Father Zorn each remaining a long term of years.

The old church that attracted so many tourists in later years was erected about 1839. Many of my readers have no doubt been shown through the old building by Margaret Boyd, an educated Indian woman, who went by the familiar name of "Aunt Margaret." She died at an advanced age in 1892. By a singular coincidence the old church which she had attended since its erection, and with which she had been so intimately connected, was torn down the same year of her death.

One of the priests, Father Lantishar, who was at the mission from 1856 to 1858, afterwards went to Northern Minnesota, and was frozen to death upon the ice while attempting to cross a lake in midwinter.

During the summer of 1884 the Franciscan Fathers were given charge of the mission. They immediately erected a number of large buildings, among them a three-story schoolhouse for the benefit of the Indian scholars, who now number about 200. The school is in charge of one of the brothers and three sisters. They are indeed doing a work of charity. The scholars get their schooling, board and clothes free of charge.

The Catholic cemetery was formerly located directly back of the church, but a few years ago every foot of space was used, and a tract of land was purchased north of the village. The old cemetery was an odd looking spot. The Indians profusely decorated the graves of their departed friends and relatives with artificial paper flowers of all kinds, which they made into wreaths and crosses, and which they also hung in great profusion upon the little whitewashed fences surrounding the mounds.

The little village which grew up about the mission was given the name of Little Traverse, taken from the French name of the bay upon which it is situated. In 1853 continuous operations relating to the village began when Richard Cooper arrived and opened a small general store. From that time the white population has had a steady growth. Since the whites have inhabited this place a number of old implements and other ancient articles have been unearthed near by, showing that this region must have been inhabited at some early date by a class of people quite highly advanced in civilization—probably the Mound Builders.

For a number of years the village was of exceptional importance, on account of its being the headquarters for the payment of the treaties made with the Indians of this section, and hundreds of the natives flocked to the place each year to receive their annuities from the government.

In 1881 the town was incorporated and the name changed to Harbor Springs, which was suggested by its two leading advantages. The town now has a population of about 2,000.

Nature has done much for Harbor Springs, and as a summer resort it has no superior. The town is growing rapidly and is bound to become one of the leading cities of northern Michigan.

CHAPEL BUILT AT LA PETITE TRAVERSE BY FATHER DE JEAN IN 1827

(FROM AN OLD DRAWING)

PETOSKEY

THE next Mission to be founded on the shores of Little Traverse Bay was at Muh-quh Se-bing (Bear River), now Petoskey, on the south side.

The Indian village on this side of the bay was originally at Muh-quh Ne-bi-sing (Bear Lake), the source of Bear River. It was founded by three Ottawa Indians, Pa-ba-ma-sha, The Sailor, A-ne-moose, Little Dog, and Moon-a-ba-tum. The first Indian to locate at the mouth of Bear River, or Bear Creek, as it is commonly called, was Sa-ga-na-kwa-do, Rising Cloud, about 1825. Shortly afterwards the village at Bear Lake was moved to the mouth of Bear River. The Indians never settled very thickly at this point on the bay. Up to 1851 nothing of importance transpired, when a few Indian families moved there from Old Mission on Grand Traverse Bay. Shortly after this Mr. P. Dougherty, who was

PETOSKEY FROM THE SOUTHEAST

conducting a Presbyterian school at Old Misson, was requested by the Indians to start a school at Bear River. He at first declined, but was afterwards prevailed upon to visit the place, which he did in 1851–2, making a favorable report to the Presbyterian Board of Missions, under whose authority he was acting. The board accordingly appointed Mr. Andrew Porter, a former teacher at Old Mission, to take charge of the new school which he did in 1852. With much difficulty he succeeded in erecting a small building on what is now the Jarman farm, west of Petoskey. Mr. Porter found the Indians kind and friendly, he never having to turn a key to prevent their stealing. He reposed the utmost confidence in them. Their principal living was "min-da-min-a-bo," or corn soup. They took great interest in their school, and many learned to read and write. After the government established Indian schools this one was adopted, and Mr. Porter was paid a salary as teacher. In 1871 the funds set apart for this purpose were exhausted and the Mission was discontinued.

In 1865 Hazen Ingalls, the first permanent white settler, arrived and purchased a little mill, which was built by a nephew of Mr. Porter in 1862. Mr.

Ingalls immediately set the mill in operation, and opened a little trading store, the first business place on the south shore of Little Traverse Bay.

The year 1873 viewed the commencement of the metropolis of the Little Traverse Region, which was named Petoskey in honor of Neyas Bedosega, an Indian, who owned all the land in the vicinity. His last name translated means "the Rising Sun," a fit name for the city that now casts its rays of influence over the entire region. The same year the postoffice was moved to the new settlement, Fox, Rose & Buttars commenced selling goods in a little log cabin and shortly afterwards the G. R. & I. Railroad was finished to this point. The general settlement of Emmet County was delayed on account of its lands being held subject to Indian treaty, but when, in 1874, the eastern townships came into market and two years later the remainder of the county was opened for settlement, the village entered upon its great career. Since that time the growth of Petoskey has been phenomenal. It is now a city of about 4,000 inhabitants and has justly been termed the "Pearl of the North."

HARBOR POINT

WHEN traveling facilities connected Little Traverse Bay with the larger cities, many tourists were attracted to its shores by the beauty of the surrounding country; resorts were established and pretty cottages erected, and each summer brought hundreds of people who sought the healthful climate and invigorating breezes of the bay.

One of the first resorts to be permanently established was on a point which curves gracefully into the bay directly in front of Harbor Springs, and which thus forms one of the best harbors on the Great Lakes. The resort was named Harbor Point.

This beautiful bit of land was first purchased from the Indians by Rev. John B. Weikamp, a Franciscan monk, who arrived from Chicago in 1855, for

NORTH SHORE OF HARBOR POINT

the purpose of establishing a mission for the Indians.   He paid $100 for the piece of ground.   He afterwards found that it was insufficient for his purpose, however, and removed to Cross Village.

The first resident at Harbor Point was C. R. Wright, of St. James, Mich., now a respected citizen of Harbor Springs.   He moved to Harbor Point in 1853 and engaged in the cooper business.   His house and shop were located near the end of the "Point."   He remained there until 1856, when he returned to St. James.

In 1878 the land was purchased by a company, incorporated as the Harbor Point Association, and opened as a resort the following year.   Harbor Point is now covered with handsome cottages, and is the pride of Little Traverse Bay.

LEGEND OF HARBOR POINT

THE Indians say that at one time Harbor Point was an island, separated from the mainland by quite an expanse of water. It was a favorite haunt for game of all kinds, as it was seldom visited by man.

During the time the "Point" was in that condition, the Indians of this region were ruled by a Great Spirit who resided on the Isle of Mackinac, and who went by the name of Potch-i-nong.

This Great Spirit possessed wonderful powers and influences and he was greatly feared by his subjects, who obeyed and honored him in all things. He ruled his people with a mighty hand and woe to him who dared disobey his commands.

Besides his earthly subjects, Potch-i-nong presided over many fairy beings who came and went at his bidding and who made his home merry with their shouts and laughter. The loveliest of these strange beings was Wa-ka-sa-mo-qua, the Great Spirit's only daughter, who was as pleasant and kind as she was beautiful. But unlike the rest of her proud companions she used to mingle with the people of the earth, much against her father's wishes. Potch-i-nong had always boasted of his fine blood and bravery and said he would rather see his daughter killed than have her marry among the mortals. She, however, continued her visits to the earth and fell in love with a young chief, Wen-de-ba-jig, handsome and brave, who resided on the mainland.

Potch-i-nong learned of the disgraceful affair, and summoning his daughter, told her that she must stop all nonsense with the young chief and thus prevent dishonor and disgrace from falling on the family. He had already given his daughter's hand to a noted Southern Motchimanitou, who was wealthy and powerful like himself, but Wa-ka-sa-mo-qua was as bent in her inclination as her father, and would not hear of her marriage to this evil one.

In vain did Potch-i-nong interpose. Wa-ka-sa-mo-qua loved Wen-de-ba-jig and did not hesitate in telling her father that she intended to marry him.

Finally Potch-i-nong, seeing that he could not dissuade his daughter, decided to have Wen-de-ba-jig put to death.

Wa-ka-sa-mo-qua learned of her father's evil determination, and when night had folded its mantle o'er the Fairy Isle, she went with all haste to her lover and informed him of what she had heard, and enveloping him in a cloud she rendered him invisible and immortal. They then embarked in a canoe and made their way to the Western shores of Me-ne-sha-ing, the small island in Little Traverse Bay, and pitched their tent.

Here they lived in happiness for many moons, but one evening when Wen-de-ba-jig had returned from the chase across the bay, his canoe loaded with the game he had slain, he was amazed to find a deep pool where his lodge had stood, and upon the bank, smiling derisively at him, was the Motchimanitou. He told Wen-de-ba-jig that he had taken his wife to dwell with him beneath the wave, but promised the pleading husband that he would return her when the island and mainland would become connected by solid ground.

Wen-de-ba-jig at once set to work upon the task that would restore to him his faithful wife, for a Great Spirit, no matter how bad, never breaks his word, and after many centuries of toil the tireless worker succeeded in making the island and mainland one, with the exception of the spot where the pool stood, which from its great depth was known as the "Devil's Pond," and the filling of which was a task beyond the power of Wen-de-ba-jig.

The Motchimanitou's voice could often be heard from the pond shouting mockingly at the indefatigable toiler, and, until the pond was filled by the refuse from the little sawmill located near by, it was necessary to quell his spirit by occasional incantations and the firing of volleys into the pond, accompanied by other ceremonies of "shooting the devil."

If the Motchimanitou was willing to accept the sawdust as solid ground the union of the long separated couple, when the last load was dumped into the pond, can be imagined.

WE-QUE-TON-SING BEACH

WE-QUE-TON-SING

WE-QUE-TON-SING is a picturesque spot one mile east of Harbor Springs. The resort comprises about 80 acres of land donated to the Presbyterians by the citizens of the latter place. In 1877 a Presbyterian committee, which met at Elkhart, Ind., accepted the gift, and the resort was established under the name of the Presbyterian Resort. The Indian name of the place was Wa-ba-bi-kang, meaning a white gravelly shore. The resort was afterwards called We-que-ton-sing, which was taken from the Indian name of Little Traverse Bay. The Indians tell no legend of the place but it is connected with their happy hunting ground in the following manner:

THE INDIAN'S HEAVEN.

Long before the paleface had ventured upon the Indian's native land, there dwelt upon the banks of Lake Michigan, near We-que-ton-sing, a squaw upwards of four score years, bent with age, who went by the name of No-ko-qua. She had a son who was the wonder of his tribe. He excelled in the chase; as a runner he could not be beaten, and in battle he always captured the most scalps. His name was Wa-sa-ko-um, which means a great light.

One night, after returning from a hunt in which he had been very successful, Wa-sa-ko-um was taken suddenly ill, and before dawn he lay unconscious upon his couch of skins.

For several days he remained thus, his aged mother constantly at his bedside, until she too, from sheer exhaustion, was compelled to lie down. She had not rested long before she was awakened by a blood-curdling war-whoop, which echoed loudly through the still night air. She arose and beheld her son arrayed in all the paraphernalia of war. Before she could catch hold of him he uttered another piercing cry and bounded out of the door. His mother, thinking that he had left his bed in a delirium, started in pursuit.

"Wa-sa-ko-um! Wa-sa-ko-um!" she cried, but Wa-sa-ko-um paid no attention to her entreaties, running only the faster. While pursuing him she noticed that he did not run upon the ground, as she did, but a little in the air.

All the rest of that night she followed him as best she could. Finally she came to a broad river in which a splashing tree seemed to say in mournful tones, "pon! pon! pon!" A little distance away she saw an Indian wigwam, to which she went and knocked. An old man made his appearance, who, in surprise asked her what she wanted. She asked him if he had seen her son.

"Yes," he replied, "I saw him. I am stationed here by Kitchi Manitou (the Great Spirit) to brain all people who may pass this way, so they can forget their worldly troubles and forever enjoy themselves in the happy hunting grounds which lie beyond the river. The noise which you hear in the water made by that large tree, is the Great Spirit's call for the dead. Your son passed here a short time ago, but being only in a trance, he could not taste the fruit which lies yonder," and he pointed to a huge strawberry, which was covered with tooth marks made by departed warriors.

"Go," he said, "and you may overtake your son, but, beware! for you are traveling on the road of the dead," and with that he left her.

No-ko-qua then started across the river. She noticed that the water beneath her was filled with minnows. Then the old man, who had just left her, seeing how hard it was for her to cross, came to assist her. While there he told her the little fishes were the souls of infants who could not cross the river, and becoming exhausted, fell into the water.

No-ko-qua followed her son for two days more, and on the second day, just as the sun was sinking, she arrived at another wigwam on the edge of a large clearing. She knocked and was admitted by a squaw as old as herself, who said she too had followed a son under similar circumstances; and, although he came every night and danced and enjoyed himself in the clearing, she could not capture him for he was really dead. She bade her guest remain with her a little while and she would show Wa-sa-ko-um to her, for she had seen him the night before.

They waited together outside the tent and just as the moon showed its silvery beams dark shadows glided into the opening, dancing and shouting to the music of the tom-tom.

One of the last to enter was a young brave who did not seem to enjoy himself as the rest, but kept clasping his hands to his head and crying, "My head is heavy! My head is heavy!"

This No-ko-qua recognized as her son, Wa-so-ko-um, whose distress was caused by his brains, which the old man stationed at the river had been unable to remove, because Wa-sa-ko-um was not dead.

No-ko-qua then did as her hostess told her, and when Wa-sa-ko-um, brushed by her she grasped him. With the help of the other old squaw she succeeded in putting him into a sack of wampum rope, which had been provided for the purpose, and bound him fast. Then by a series of sweats they brought him back to consciousness.

No-ko-qua and her son remained with their kind hostess some time, watching the festivities of the dead each night, but as they were unable to share in their happiness, they returned to the land of the living, and Wa-sa-ko-um never tired till the day he died, of relating his experience in the happy hunting ground.

The Ottawas still cherish many superstitions based on this legend. They pick the strawberry with the utmost reluctance, because the legend says it was the fruit of life; and they never kill little minnows because their fathers thought they were the souls of departed children.

BAY VIEW FROM THE NORTHEAST

BAY VIEW

BAY VIEW "the beautiful" has the distinctive honor of attracting more visitors each summer than any other resort on Little Traverse Bay. Students from all parts of the world come to her classic shores, where they can enjoy a peaceful vacation, combining pleasure and education, as her facilities for both are unsurpassed.

The resort was established in 1875, the land having been selected by a committee from the M. E. conference and donated to the Methodists by the citizens of Petoskey. The dedicatory sermon was delivered by Dr. Pilcher the following year.

When the Indians are told of Bay View's educational advantages, they only laugh and say: "No wonder, that was the home of Ne-bwa-ka-o-ge-ma."

Ne-bwa-ka-o-ge-ma was a very learned Indian, his name signifying the wise chieftain. Although the most of his people resided on the north side of the bay, Bay View seemed to have a strange fascination for him, and he built himself a house there and called it " Ba-she-kan-da-quck ne wig-wam," which means "my beautiful home."

Often after he had returned from the chase Ne-bwa-ka-o-ge-ma would sit on the shore near his wigwam and watch the setting sun and after night had spread her sable folds he would meditate on the moon and stars. It is related of him that he composed poetry which he took great delight in reciting to his subjects.

The following stanza, which has been handed down from generation to generation among the Indians, is said to have been composed by Ne-bwa-ka-o-ge-ma:

Anawe awe waiabine wingwed

Agimakang jajaie nindakimina,

Aka dash wi wika odamakasin

Wadashi minawanigo kioseiang.

TRANSLATION.

Although the cruel paleface
In our land can now be found,
He will never find a place
In our happy hunting ground.

He was found dead one morning on the beach, where he had remained all night trying to make out what the stars were.

He was buried near the spot he loved so well, amid the sorrow of his entire tribe.

7

ROARING BROOK NEAR ITS MOUTH

LEGEND OF.....

ROARING BROOK

ROARING BROOK is the youngest of the Little Traverse Bay resorts, having been opened in 1894 by a number of Lansing capitalists, but it is by no means the least promising. It is situated one and one-half miles east of Harbor Springs, and has the most picturesque view of any resort on the bay. The Indians tell the following legend of the beautiful little stream which courses through the grounds, and from which the resort derives its name:

Years and years ago, where the pretty town of Harbor Springs now stands and scattered along the shores of Little Traverse Bay, was a quaint little Indian village. Game and fish were plenty, the wigwams of the inhabitants were adorned with the best and softest of furs, and contentment and happiness reigned supreme. They were ruled over by a chief who was supposed to possess

SCENE ON LITTLE TRAVERSE BAY NEAR MOUTH OF ROARING BROOK

supernatural powers, and the Great Spirit had blessed him with an extremely beautiful daughter whose hand was sought by all the young braves of the village, among whom was Neoma, a young man who was considered the best warrior and hunter in the tribe.

Winona, the chief's daughter, returned the young man's affections, but Neoma had a rival, Motchimanitou, an evil spirit, who dwelt in the vicinity of Roaring Brook and whom the chief wished his daughter to marry, hoping thereby to gain more power and influence.

Neoma asked the chief for his daughter's hand, but was rejected and Winona was imprisoned in a separate wigwam with guards placed at the entrance, so that the lovers might not elope.

But 'tis said that "Love laughs at locksmiths," and so one dark night Neoma stole into Winona's prison, first drugging the guards with a potion he had obtained from an old witch who resided on the outskirts of the village. Winona was only too glad to regain her freedom and join her faithful lover. They embarked in a birch bark canoe, which Neoma had provided for the occasion, and fled to an island far out in Lake Michigan, where the twain landed, pitched their tent, and for a time lived happily together.

But Motchimanitou, being an evil spirit, soon learned the whereabouts of Neoma and his bride, and one day when Neoma was in quest of game, hied himself to the secret wigwam and abducted the winsome Winona, whom he carried to his home—a dull, dark cave in the woods near Roaring Brook—where he imprisoned her.

Neoma soon returned home, and missing his bride, spent many weary hours of anguish, but at last surmised the cause of her disappearance. He immediately started in pursuit of Motchimanitou but arrived at the latter's rendezvous too late to rescue Winona and was only met by the jeers and mocking laughter of Motchimanitou. With a heavy heart he lingered about Winona's prison, contriving many plans by which he might rescue her, but he failed in all his attempts.

Meanwhile Winona became heart-broken and despondent and she shed many tears. She rapidly failed in health, until she was only a mere skeleton of her former self, and in a short time she crossed "the dark river of death."

Neoma was overwhelmed with grief, and disheartened he climbed one of the high trees near where Motchimanitou dwelt, and with a weird, plaintive death song threw himself to the foot, over 75 feet below, striking in the waters of Roaring Brook, which upon his death, caught up the sad air and ever since has murmured the death song of the departed warrior, which noise has given rise to the name of "Roaring" Brook.

ROARING BROOK INN

OLD INDIAN CEMETERY AT CROSS VILLAGE

CROSS VILLAGE

CROSS VILLAGE is situated on Lake Michigan, about 16 miles northwest of Harbor Springs, and is a small town of about 325 inhabitants, mostly Indians. The popular belief is that the first mission there was established by Pere Marquette, but this is not known for a certainty. Probably the formation of the belief lies in the fact that the Indians say it was established by "Kitchimekatewikwanaie," the Great Priest.

When the explorers first landed at Cross Village, a large cedar cross was erected on the hill, from which the town derived its French name, *La Croix*, in Indian A-na-mi-a-wa-tig-on-ing. The Indians say it was placed by their request over the grave of a chief whom they greatly loved. The old cross has long ago succumbed to the elements and another erected in its place, about two rods from where the first cross stood. This one also has been replaced several times, so that it would be impossible to find the exact position of the first cross. The present one is probably the fifth or sixth.

Who the priest was that first had charge of the *La Croix* mission is not known. Indian traditions say that the first priest at *La Croix* was well liked and converted many of their number. It was probably Rev. Father du Jaunay. He stayed at *La Croix* nearly one year, and thinking that he had sufficiently civilized the Indians, he decided with their aid, to celebrate Corpus Christi in an appropriate manner. A large number of the L'Arbre Croche mission Indians were invited to attend the ceremony. They arrived at *La Croix* the evening previous. During the night two Indians became involved in a quarrel over a girl. The members of the two missions took sides and a terrible massacre ensued in which ten braves were killed. When morning came the priest gazed in horror on the dead bodies, and washing his hands of the affair, he embarked in a canoe and left the spot forever.

When the Catholics returned and re-established the abandoned missions in the Little Traverse region in 1825, a church was built at *La Croix* by Father

De Jean. The history that is left of the mission is very meagre. The village at that time was located below the hill.

The old church which now stands near the center of the village, was erected about 1848 by Father Mrak. The last priest to have charge of the mission was Father Sifferath in 1868.

In 1875 the name of the town was changed from *La Croix* to Cross Village.

REV. JOANNES BERN. WEIKAMP
(FOUNDER OF CROSS VILLAGE CONVENT)

CROSS VILLAGE CONVENT

IN the springtime of 1854 there arrived at Little Traverse a small Mackinaw sail boat, carrying a Catholic priest and a few brothers and sisters of the order of St. Francis. The villagers gazed at them in wonder as they landed. The priest, Rev. Father John B. Weikamp, informed them that he intended to establish a convent in their midst, and wished to buy some of their land.

Father Weikamp was a German by birth, having emigrated from Prussia in 1850. He had lately been at the head of a large Catholic institution in Chicago, but his building having burned down, he decided to labor as a missionary among the Indians. After he had been at Little Traverse some time he decided to purchase Harbor Point and offered the Indians $100 for the piece of ground.

CROSS VILLAGE CONVENT

After much parleying the Indians accepted the proposition, but after the purchase had been made Father Weikamp thought the land insufficient for his purpose and tried to purchase more. The rest of the land in the vicinity, however, was held in trust for the Indians and could not be bought. Father Weikamp therefore went to Cross Village and purchased a tract of 2,000 acres from an Indian. In the spring of 1855 he and his followers removed to that place and began the construction of the large wooden building which has since been known as the Cross Village Convent.

Father Weikamp himself superintended the work, but the manual labor was done almost entirely by the Indians. By January it was nearly completed, and several more brethren and sisters were added to their small congregation. The organization was entitled the Benevolent, Charitable and Religious Society of St. Francis, in honor of their patron saint.

For many years the society thrived. Land was cleared, a gristmill, sawmill and shops were erected, besides a parochial school for Indian children. The priests were excellent farmers, and the crops and stock they raised made the convent self-supporting. Up to the time the convent was closed, anyone desiring to know anything about Emmet County farming was always directed to the Cross Village Convent as evidence of the good farming qualities of our soil.

For about 35 years Father Weikamp remained monarch of his little domain, daily making three hours of meditation before a skull and cross bones placed on a sepulcher, which he always kept in readiness for his remains. Visitors to the convent were always treated courteously by the kind-hearted monk.

Since the death of Father Weikamp, a few years ago, however, the society steadily dwindled in numbers, and in the fall of 1894 the convent was closed, the members going to Joliet, Ill., the headquarters of the Franciscan order.

In the spring of 1895 the work of destroying the old land mark began, when Rev. Father Anthony, who had made it his home for 35 years, purchased the property and with the approval of the entire region, decided to preserve what was left of the famous old building.

BEAVER ISLAND .... AND ITS .... MORMON KINGDOM

BY CHAS. J. STRANG, ONE OF "KING" STRANG'S SONS

BEAVER ISLAND, the largest in Lake Michigan, lies about thirty miles northwest of Little Traverse Bay. From 1850 to 1856 this island was the headquarters of a band of people who assumed for themselves rights and prerogatives contrary to the spirit of our constitution and laws, and whose acts made a considerable portion of the history of the Traverse region for that decade. The rise and fall of the "kingdom" which then flourished there will always be a prolific subject for writers who visit this northern country.

These people called themselves "Latter Day Saints," but they were better

JAMES J. STRANG

(FROM THE ONLY PHOTOGRAPH OF HIM KNOWN TO BE IN EXISTENCE).

known as Mormons.   Their leader was James J. Strang, who called himself a "king," and assumed many of the prerogatives of a monarch.

Mr. Strang was born in Scipio, N. Y., March 21, 1813, but grew to manhood in Chautauqua County.   His education was obtained in the public schools of the county, closing with a course in the Fredonia Academy.   He studied law, and was admitted to the bar.   In 1843 he settled in Burlington, Wis., and some time before the death of Joseph Smith, in 1844, he visited Nauvoo and became a Mormon.   After Smith's death, Strang disputed with Brigham Young the right to lead the church, and succeeded in gathering quite a large following at his "stake of Zion" in Wisconsin.   In 1847 he visited Beaver Island, and decided to establish his people there, founding the village of St. James, which was named in honor of himself.   On July 8, 1850, he reorganized his church and established the "kingdom," and from that day he was known as "King Strang."   His authority was respected and obeyed by the "Saints," and as cheerfully hated and opposed by the "Gentiles."   He controlled the Mormon vote, and was elected to the Legislature of 1853, and again in 1855. The practice of "consecration" led to many conflicts between the Mormons and Gentile fishermen in that vicinity. Such expressions as "The earth is the Lord's, and the fullness thereof," and, "We are the Lord's chosen people," stilled the consciences and justified the use of property lawfully owned by others, yet it is undoubtedly true that many depredations were committed by irresponsible persons and deliberately charged to the Mormons.

Mr. Strang had frequent collisions with the authorities at Mackinac, but with his knowledge of the law, and his readiness in debate, he cleared himself from every charge. At one time the Sheriff of Mackinac County hunted him three days in the wilds of the island with a posse of ten whites and thirty Indians, and offered a reward of $300 for his body, dead or alive, but Mr. Strang eluded them and avoided arrest.

In the spring of 1856 matters reached a crisis. A resident of the island, Mr. Thomas Bedford, had been publicly flogged by Mr. Strang's authority, and he determined to have revenge. He enlisted the support of a few others, among them Mr. Alex. Wentworth, and they decided to kill Mr. Strang. The opportunity came on June 20, when the U. S. steamer Michigan was in the harbor at St. James, Strang was fatally shot, after which Bedford, Wentworth, and some

RESIDENCE OF JAMES J. STRANG ON BEAVER ISLAND FROM 1850 TO 1856

others were taken to Mackinac, "tried," and acquitted. After the acquittal, Bedford and his friends organized a company at Mackinac and other points near the islands, and returned to St. James and drove from their homes every Mormon except a very few who were willing to renounce their religion. Strang's house and printing office were ransacked and robbed of everything of value; the tabernacle was destroyed, and the property of the Mormons confiscated and divided among the raiders. Warning was served on the Mormons to leave the island within a specified time. The warning was heeded, a few going to the mainland near Charlevoix, but the main body proceeded to Milwaukee and Chicago. Mr. Strang was removed to Wisconsin, where he died July 9, 1856.

Strang's house, which has been raised by recent writers to the dignity of a "royal palace," was substantially built of hewn logs, and after the dispersion of the Mormons it became the mecca of relic hunters, and so continued until 1892, when it was destroyed by fire.

Of the present residents of the village of St. James, the majority are Irish Catholics, many of them having gone there directly from Ireland. The principal occupation of the people is fishing, and they live happy and contented in their island home.

AN INDIAN LAWSUIT

SOMETIME during the year 1830, Dun-a-age-ee, an Indian, killed his niece, a beautiful girl of sixteen summers, near Seven Mile Point.

The Indians knew that Dun-a-age-ee had committed a terrible crime, and the friends of the young girl wished to punish him as the white people did their criminals, but as they had no method in their native customs of disposing of such cases, except by barbaric forms, they went for advice to Col. Boyd, a white haired veteran of the war of the revolution, who resided at Mackinac Island, and who had much influence among them. Mr. Boyd, fearing to make enemies of Dun-a-age-ee's friends, told the Indians he would have nothing to do with the matter and advised them to mete out to the prisoner whatever punishment they found he deserved by some proceedings of their own.

After much consultation, the chiefs decided to hold a lawsuit. So a large wigwam was built on the bluff near Seven Mile Point and all the relatives of the murderer and his victim assembled and also a number of onlookers.

On either side of the tent were long benches, the relatives of Dun-a-age-ee on one side, and those of the murdered girl on the other, the oldest member of the family being seated at the head and so on down.

At the head of the tent on an elevated platform, sat A-pock-o-ze-gun, the great chief of the Ottawas, his person ornamented with feathers and beads and wearing his beautifully embroidered blanket, as was customary at great events. In the center of the tent were great piles of furs, blankets, butts of tobacco, guns, ammunition, etc. Outside were horses, cattle, in fact, everything that the Indians considered wealth, brought there by the relatives of Dun-a-age-ee to buy their kinsman's liberty.

When the time for the trial arrived Chief A-pock-o-ze-gun arose and made a short, eloquent speech in his native tongue. He said they were not gathered to avenge the murdered girl, as their priest told them God would do that; but they were there for the purpose of making peace between the estranged kinsmen.

He then produced a caluma (long pipe), from one of the medicine men present, and, filling it with tobacco lit it by a flint and steel. After he had taken a long puff he presented it to the first of Dun-a-age-ee's relatives, his father, who smoked it as a token of peace.

The chief said, "Me-sa-gwa-uck," which means "that's right," and passed it to the next man, who likewise took a puff, and so on, to the end of that row.

The chief then passed the pipe to the first one on the other side; a girl, who, after some hesitation, took it and smoked. All followed her example, down to the first of two of the girl's brothers, who sat at the upper end. The brother shook his head and said "kaw" (no).

The chief muttered "too bad," and taking the pipe, emptied it of its contents. Then he refilled it, and lighting it, handed it to the last brother.

"Kaw! kaw!" he said, indignantly, and turning to his other brothers and sisters, who had smoked the pipe of peace, he rebuked them fiercely, saying that for those few articles they were willing to sacrifice their sister's life, but that he would not rest till he had killed the villain.

The friends of Dun-a-age-ee advised him to fly lest the brother kill him, and he accordingly left for the Saginaws, where he remained until the man who had sworn the vendetta was dead.

THE SEA SERPENT

BESIDES its natural beauties and historical interest, Little Traverse Bay presents another attraction of a peculiar nature which in late years has caused much interest throughout the country. We have reference to the famous sea serpent. The Indians have always claimed that some great marine monster inhabited the bay, but, of course, as these people are very superstitious, their belief should be given little credence. Yet the appearance of some strange creature in the waters of the bay may have had something to do with the origin of their legend.

Several times in late years different persons claim to have seen while in a boat and oftentimes from the shore a great monster in the bay.

On one occasion while a steamer was carrying a crowd of pleasure seekers from Petoskey to Charlevoix, a large number of the excursionists viewed together what appeared to be a long serpent making its way at a rapid rate through the water.

Many people, however, disclaim the stories and say it is all imagination. But if people are subject to optical illusions, the camera is not. The accompanying picture of the serpent was taken from the steam ferry "Adrienne" while crossing the bay from Petoskey to Harbor Springs in June, 1895. That it was not a log is vouchsafed for by the fact that it disappeared from view as the boat approached it. Whether the object was a living thing or not remains a mystery.

Some of the people residing upon the bay, whose enthusiasm got the better of their judgment, obtained a distorted log and tried to palm it off as the sea serpent, but the object seen so many times in the waters of Little Traverse Bay, is something of a far different nature than an ordinary log.

No doubt imagination has had much to do with this sea serpent, but it would not be very surprising if a marine monster of some description had taken a particular fancy to the surroundings of the bay and had made it his home, allowing himself to be seen just often enough to arouse the curiosity of the people.

THE INDIAN COMPANY

ONE of the interesting features of the late Civil War was a company of Indian soldiers who fought under Grant from the battle of the Wilderness until the surrender of the Confederates at Appomattox Court House. "Company K, First Michigan Sharpshooters," was composed almost entirely of Indians from the Little Traverse Region. Of the 100 men who left to fight for their country, scarcely half that number returned. The company was organized at Little Traverse in 1863 by Lieut. G. A. Graveraet, a gallant young soldier, who fell mortally wounded in the battle before Petersburg, after digging a grave for his father who fell by his side.

Letters received home from superior officers stated that the Indians were among the best soldiers in the service. They entered each battle with vim and vigor and fought as gallantly for that same country under the stars and stripes as their ancestors did when they defended it from the whites under the feathers of the wild American Eagle.

WEOSMA: A TALE OF THE OTTAWAS

IN READMOND township, 'neath the wide spreading boughs of a large oak, is a mound which marks the last resting place of one of the noble red men of the forest.

Having heard that there was a story connected with the one whose remains were interred beneath the sod, the writer asked an old native who resided near by if he could inform him of the circumstances of the case. "Bad story; me tell you," replied the old Indian, and as he lighted his pipe I sat down on a log beside him while he related the following sad tale:

During the palmiest days of the Ottawa Indians, when their arrows brought the crimson blood spouting forth from many a wild deer and their war-whoops sent terror to the hearts of the braves of contemporary tribes, Weosma, a brave warrior and hunter, whose aim was perfect and whose foot was as light as a fleeting deer's, resided with his aged mother among a peaceful clan of these Indians who had pitched their tents where Cross Village now stands.

All the young maidens of the village vied with each other in trying to win this brave young hunter's hand, but he was heedless to their attentions and lived happily in the company of his mother. But as Cupid was not absent, only sleeping, the wanting one at last appeared and awoke the nymph of love to his highest pitch, and Weosma was a victim as helpless as any ever was before.

His enamorate was Enewah, the bewitching daughter of a great chief who ruled over the tribe in the region of Little Traverse. Weosma had first met her while on a hunting expedition and ever after that eventful day his life was not the same; he was unhappy when out of her company and he exerted himself in performing brave deeds that he might be worthy of Enewah's love. Enewah in turn looked with favor upon his attentions and their wedding day was fixed, and all looked bright and promising for the future life of the happy couple. But like the adder that stingeth in the dark, an evil one appeared upon the scene, who by the fertility of a revengeful brain, forever blighted their happy life.

Amo, a rejected suitor of Enewah's, had sworn revenge upon the fair young maiden, and now came a glorious opportunity to carry out his vendetta.

Great preparations had been made for the wedding day. As Weosma was a very popular young man, all the chiefs and medicine men of the tribe were to hold a great feast in honor of his success. The evening previous to the great occasion Amo arrived at Enewah's wigwam in breathless haste and warned the girl not to marry a young man who was already betrothed to a woman of another tribe, which, to the Ottawas, was a great crime. Enewah only laughed in scorn at Amo's scheme and turned away, saying that Weosma was too good a man to do anything of that sort. Then Amo told the story to her father, the great chief, who thinking him his friend, forbid his daughter marrying such a scoundrel as Weosma was proven to be.

When Weosma arrived at Enewah's wigwam that evening to finish preparations for the next day, the chief received him very coldly and told him what he had heard. Excuses were of no avail and after a few words Weosma was ordered out of his sight forever.

In despair the young man returned home. Little did he sleep that night. The next morning bright and early he took down his bow and quiver of arrows and started for the woods. He returned shortly, however, with two spotless white pigeons, which he threw upon the ground before his mother, saying: "Mother, I am as innocent of the crime of which I am accused as are those pigeons; I know you will believe me if no one else will. Those are the last birds I will ever shoot for you," and with that he drove his hunting knife to his heart and expired. He was buried near the place where he killed the pigeons, and the mound now marks the spot.

The news of his death spread throughout the tribe, and the gay throng that was to gather in *fete* on the morrow was turned into one of sorrow and disappointment.

When the chief heard of the story of the two pigeons he at once summoned Amo, but the latter, thinking the truth would be discovered, had fled from the country.

Enewah, who had cherished the hope that her lover might be proven innocent in the sight of her father, became almost frantic at the sad news. She rapidly pined away, and finally ended her earthly existence by the same hunting knife that had killed her lover, with these words: "Bama, bama pe ning ga wa ba ma," which translated mean, "I will see him bye-and-bye."

As he finished speaking the old man's eyes filled with tears, and he bowed his head in sorrow at the recollection of one of the saddest tragedies that ever blighted the history of his happy ancestors.

THE END